W9-BNU-698

ADOLF
HITLER
DICTATOR OF NAZI GERMANY

SPECIAL LIVES IN HISTORY THAT BECOME

Signature LIVES

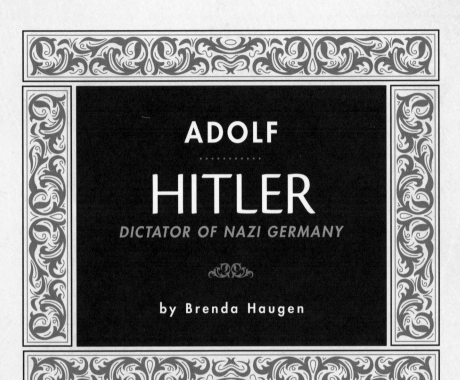

ADOLF
HITLER
DICTATOR OF NAZI GERMANY

by Brenda Haugen

Content Adviser: Harold Marcuse, Ph.D.,
Department of History,
University of California, Santa Barbara

Reading Adviser: Rosemary G. Palmer, Ph.D.,
Department of Literacy, College of Education,
Boise State University

COMPASS POINT BOOKS ✦ MINNEAPOLIS, MINNESOTA

Compass Point Books
3109 West 50th Street, #115
Minneapolis, MN 55410

Visit Compass Point Books on the Internet at *www.compasspointbooks.com*
or e-mail your request to *custserv@compasspointbooks.com*

Editor: Sue Vander Hook
Page Production: Noumenon Creative
Photo Researcher: Marcie C. Spence
Cartographer: XNR Productions, Inc.
Library Consultant: Kathleen Baxter

Art Director: Jaime Martens
Creative Director: Keith Griffin
Editorial Director: Carol Jones
Managing Editor: Catherine Neitge

In memory of Lisa Babb Gross. *BLH*

Library of Congress Cataloging-in-Publication Data
Haugen, Brenda
  Adolf Hitler, Dictator of Nazi Germany / by Brenda Haugen.
    p. cm.—(Signature lives)
  Includes bibliographical references and index.
  ISBN 0-7565-1589-0 (hard cover)
  1. Adolf Hitler, 1889–1945—Juvenile literature. 2. Heads of state—
Germany—Biography—Juvenile literature. 3. Germany—History—
1933–1945—Juvenile literature. 4. World War, 1939–1945—Juvenile
literature. I. Title. II. Series.
  DD247.H5H3235 2006
  943.086092—dc22   2005025089

Signature Lives

MODERN WORLD

From 1900 to the present day, humanity and the world have undergone major changes. New political ideas resulted in worldwide wars. Fascism and communism divided some countries, and democracy brought others together. Drastic shifts in theories and practice tested the standards of personal freedoms and religious conventions as well as science, technology, and industry. These changes have created a need for world policies and an understanding of international relations. The new mind-set of the modern world includes a focus on humanitarianism and the belief that a global economy has made the world a more connected place.

Table of Contents

1 On the World's Stage

❧❀❧

The world's attention was focused on Germany in 1936. The capital city of Berlin was host of the Summer and Winter Olympic Games. But German Chancellor Adolf Hitler was not a big fan of the Olympics. International competition only caused pure-blooded, blond, blue-eyed Germans—Aryans, as he called them—to mix with what he considered the lesser peoples of the world.

His propaganda minister, Joseph Goebbels, argued that the Olympics would provide the perfect stage for Germany. The Games, he said, would show the world that Hitler was right about the superiority of Aryan athletes and prove how great Germany was. These Games would be the first to be televised on a closed-circuit system in Germany. The audience

Adolf Hitler saluted the athletes at the 1936 Olympic Games in Berlin, Germany.

would be larger than ever before. Big screens would be set up in theaters throughout the city so local residents could view the games free of charge. Hitler was easily convinced.

Work began on a beautiful stadium large enough to seat more than 100,000 spectators. Hitler said, "If Germany is to stand host to the entire world, her preparations must be complete and magnificent."

Even though Hitler was now convinced the Games should go on in Germany, others weren't sure. In fact, some were dead set against it. The International Olympic Committee (IOC) had chosen Berlin in 1931, before Hitler had come to power. Now things were different in Germany.

When Hitler became the country's chancellor—the second in command—on January 30, 1933, he made changes almost overnight. He no longer allowed basic civil rights such as freedom of speech and freedom of the press. In March, the first concentration camp opened in Dachau in southern Germany. At first, it served as a prison for those who disagreed with Hitler and his beliefs. Then Jews especially were singled out for imprisonment and torture. Outside the camps, Jews

Berlin had been the site chosen for the 1916 Olympics. However, that wasn't to be. World War I (1914–1918) caused the 1916 Games to be canceled. Because of its role in starting the war, Germany wasn't allowed to participate in the Games again until 1928.

were persecuted in other ways, from boycotts of their businesses to loss of jobs and citizenship. By the time of the Olympics, more than 70 prisoners had been killed in Dachau, about two every month.

The barracks and ammunition factory in a 1933 photo of Dachau concentration camp in Dachau, Germany

People in other nations knew this was going on. Many tried to get their countries to boycott the Berlin Olympics. However, the Games went on as planned, with a record 49 countries participating. Among them was the United States, which fielded the largest team after Germany.

The world wanted to see how Hitler would handle the Games. Would the German team include any Jews? By this time, Jewish Germans were banned from most grocery stores and restaurants, as well as public swimming pools, sports clubs, ski slopes, beaches, and other places in Germany. How would athletes from other countries be treated? The U.S. team included 18 African-Americans, whom Hitler considered subhumans along with Jews.

It was obvious throughout Germany that rules were different for Jews, a prejudice called anti-Semitism. Signs alongside the roads condemned and humiliated Jews and encouraged the boycott of their businesses. Representatives of the IOC didn't want the world to see these signs during the Olympics. At first, Hitler refused to remove them. He said the German

In 1935, anti-Semitic signs were erected throughout Germany. Some stated, "Jews not wanted in this place!"

people had the right to express their feelings. But he backed down after the head of the IOC said that either the signs came down or the Olympics would be canceled.

Hitler ordered the anti-Semitic signs in Berlin to be taken down, and Germany proceeded to make a huge spectacle of the Olympics. Olympic flags flew from housetops as the festivities began in a crowded Berlin. Musical fanfares greeted the arrival of Hitler to the huge sports complex as the German crowd saluted him. With one arm stretched toward him, they shouted, *"Heil, Hitler!"* (Hail, Hitler!).

While Germany won more medals than any other country, the undisputed star of the Games was

Amateur Athletic Union President Jeremiah Mahoney tried to get the United States to take a stand against the German government's persecution of its Jewish citizens. He asked that the American team boycott the 1936 Olympics in Berlin. U.S. Olympic Committee President Avery Brundage took the opposing view, saying politics shouldn't have any place in such sporting events. In the end, Brundage won, and the United States took part in the Games.

Jesse Owens. This exceptional African-American runner earned four gold medals. Despite the victories of Owens and other black athletes, Hitler still believed Aryan athletes were superior. "The Americans ought to be ashamed of themselves for letting their medals be won by Negroes," Hitler said to the leader of his youth organization, Baldur von Schirach.

At first, Hitler shook hands with athletes after

their victories, but he refused to meet with Owens. When Hitler was told he should either shake hands with all the winners or with none, Hitler chose none. "Do you really think that I will allow myself to be photographed shaking hands with a Negro?" he asked Schirach.

Despite Hitler's behavior, the Olympics improved Germany's image. The country showed its prosperous, friendly side. That August, foreign news correspondent William Shirer wrote in his diary:

> I'm afraid the Nazis have succeeded with their propaganda. First, the Nazis have run the games on a lavish scale never before experienced, and this has appealed to the athletes. Second, the Nazis have put up a very good front for the general visitors, especially the big businessmen.

During the Games, Jewish Germans had some relief from persecution. But when the international event ended, so did any peace they may have experienced. As soon as the Games were over, Captain Wolfgang Furstner, a Jewish German in charge of the Olympic village, was dismissed from the German military. Two days later, he killed himself. Gretel Bergmann, a Jewish German athlete who tied the German record in the high jump, was denied a future spot on the German Olympic team. She left

her homeland in 1937 and moved to the United States to escape persecution.

Like Bergmann, many Jewish Germans fled to other countries after the Games. But most Jews would not be so fortunate. Many countries wouldn't let them in. Eventually, more than 6 million Jews and others Hitler considered not worthy of living, such as gypsies and the physically and mentally disabled, would be mass murdered during the reign of terror of this German dictator. ℘

The German, U.S., and Italian relay teams stood before the 1936 Olympic crowd at a medal ceremony in Berlin, Germany. The U.S. team composed of Ralph Metcalfe, Jesse Owens, Foy Draper, and Frank Wyckoff won the gold.

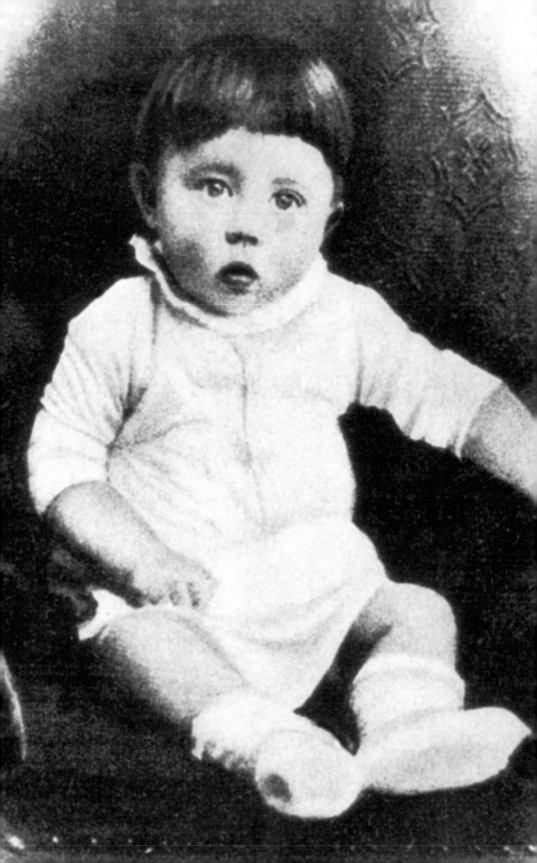

2 GROWING UP ANGRY

Chapter

೧৬✕৬৩

Adolf Hitler was born on April 20, 1889, in Braunau am Inn, Austria-Hungary, a town on the border of Austria and Germany. His family history and even his last name were sometimes confusing.

Adolf's grandmother, Maria Schicklgruber, was 42 years old and unmarried in 1837 when she gave birth to Adolf's father, Alois. Five years later, Maria married a man named Georg Hiedler. When Maria died in 1849, Alois went to live with Hiedler's brother Nepomuk and his family. When Alois was 19, Georg died.

Alois was 39 years old when he decided to list Georg Hiedler as his father on his birth record. Now, Alois Schicklgruber officially became Alois Hitler, a common alternate spelling of Hiedler. At times, it was also spelled Hittler or Hüttler.

Adolf Hitler as a baby

By now, Alois had moved up from an apprentice shoemaker to a well-respected member of the Austrian customs service in Braunau, on the Inn River. He inspected goods traded between Austria and Germany. By the time he was 47, his first two wives had died, and he married his third wife, Klara Pölzl, who was 20 years younger. When they were married in 1885, Klara was already pregnant with his child.

Klara and Alois soon had two children. A third child lived only a few days. Just months after the newborn's death, the Hitler family suffered more tragedy. The two toddlers were struck with a deadly bacterial disease of the throat called diphtheria. Neither child survived.

Klara Pölzl Hitler (1860–1907), mother of Adolf Hitler

When Klara gave birth to her fourth child, Adolf, on April 20, 1889, she feared he would also die. She worried about him constantly. Klara spoiled Adolf, who was clearly her favorite, even after he was joined by siblings Edmund and Paula. Alois was stricter and more demanding of Adolf. Paula later said:

It was especially my brother Adolf, who challenged my father to extreme harshness and who got his sound thrashing every day. How often on the other hand did my mother caress him and try to obtain with her kindness, where the father could not succeed with harshness!

At the age of 6, Adolf started school and proved to be a bright student. He liked to read, especially stories about cowboys and Indians. He particularly enjoyed drawing. Learning history also intrigued him. But when he was about to start another year of school, his father retired and moved the family to a small farm in Leonding.

Alois Hitler (1837–1903), father of Adolf Hitler

Alois wanted Adolf to follow in his footsteps and work for the Austrian government. Adolf wasn't sure what he wanted to become, but he knew he didn't want to be an office worker like his father. Alois continued to try to persuade him. He told his son stories about how much he enjoyed his work, but Adolf barely listened.

Adolf later wrote:

> *I yawned and grew sick to my stomach at the thought of sitting in an office, deprived of my liberty; ceasing to be the master of my own time and being compelled to force the content of a whole life into blanks that had to be filled out.*

Adolf's dream was to become an artist, which made his father angry. Adolf reacted:

> *My father forbade me to nourish the slightest hope of ever being allowed to study art. I went one step further and declared that if that was the case I would stop studying altogether.*

And that's what he did. At the age of 12, he started failing his classes because of what his teachers called a lack of diligence. Adolf explained:

> *For the moment only one thing was certain: my obvious lack of success at school. What gave me pleasure I learned, especially everything which, in my opinion, I should later need as a painter. What seemed to me unimportant … I sabotaged completely.*

On January 3, 1903, Adolf's father died. Now at the age of 13, Adolf had more freedom to plan his

Adolf Hitler (back center) with his fellow schoolmates in Lambach, Austria, in 1899

future. He continued to struggle in school and spent more and more time at home reading and drawing.

At the age of 16, Adolf convinced his mother to let him drop out of school. For a while, he lived a life of leisure and spent his time reading, drawing, and painting. In the evenings, he often attended musical and theatrical performances. He especially liked grand operas by Richard Wagner about myths of German history.

Eventually, Adolf pursued the dream his father had tried to discourage. He decided he would become an artist. ❧

3 FAILURE IN VIENNA

❦⟨❀⟩❦

Eighteen-year-old Adolf Hitler set out from Leonding in 1907 to visit the Academy of Fine Arts in Vienna, the capital of Austria-Hungary. He wanted to take the admission test for the General School of Painting. Although his beloved mother was now weak and fragile and suffering gravely with cancer, she encouraged him to go. Hitler set out on his trip, convinced it would be what he called child's play to pass the examination.

He was wrong. The examiners found Hitler's art good enough to allow him to take the drawing test. But since he didn't draw many faces, they suggested that he go to architecture school instead. Still, Hitler held fast to his dream. He was convinced he could be a painter, and he didn't want to take the technical

Adolf Hitler's watercolor painting of a church and castle in
Perchtoldsdorf, a small town southeast of Vienna, Austria

courses needed to become an architect.

Disappointed by his failure, Hitler went home to care for his ailing mother. He didn't tell her that he had failed the test. Klara died on December 21, 1907, and Hitler was devastated.

He later wrote:

The death of my mother put a sudden end to all my high-flown plans. … It was a dreadful blow, particularly for me. I had honored my father, but my mother I had loved.

In February 1908, Hitler returned to Vienna and lived in an apartment with his best friend, August Kubizek, who joined him there to study music. Hitler kept on drawing and applied to take the entrance exam at the art school once again. But this time, his art wasn't even good enough to get him into the actual test.

Hitler felt humiliated. Ashamed at his second failure, he packed his things and moved out of his apartment without telling anyone. He rented a room for a while but eventually ended up living on the streets.

By 1909, Hitler was working at odd jobs or begging for money to survive. Dressed in dirty, torn clothes, he slept in parks or homeless shelters. "Even now I shudder when I think of those pitiful dens, the shelters and lodging houses, those sinister pictures of dirt and repugnant filth," he later wrote.

His situation improved in 1910. With the encouragement of a new friend, Reinhold Hanisch, a drifter from Berlin, Hitler painted postcards of famous buildings in Vienna. Hanisch found people who would buy them. Hitler moved into a more stable home for single men. Encouraged by his modest success, he began painting and selling larger pieces

A watercolor painting found in the cellar of an Iranian building is attributed to Adolf Hitler. It is believed to have been painted in Vienna in 1911 or 1912.

of art. He created scenes of landscapes and buildings but rarely painted faces.

Hitler later said the men's home was where he started developing his anti-Semitic views. He read pamphlets and newspapers that praised the white northern Aryan peoples as superior to everyone else. Although he was exposed to such ideas before, they now took root in his heart. He began dreaming of creating a nation of Aryans, a pure German race, and ridding the world of Jews and other people he considered undesirable.

Hitler turned 21 that year and began avoiding required military service in the Austrian army. He wanted to flee to Germany, whose culture he idolized. However, he wanted to wait for an inheritance that his father had left for him. He had to turn 24 in order to get the money. Three years passed, and he finally received the inheritance check. On May 24, 1913, he left Vienna behind. Later, he reflected on his time there:

> *I had set foot in this town while still half a boy and I left it a man, grown quiet and grave. In it I obtained the foundations for a broad world view and a particular political outlook that ... never left me.*

The word anti-Semitism was first used by a German journalist in 1879 to describe some political groups in Germany that wanted to exclude Jewish Germans from public life. The term was soon used in other countries as well. It now refers to all forms of hostility toward Jews and the Jewish religion since ancient times. Even some ancient Greeks did not like Jews because they believed in only one God.

Hitler may have been looking at the world in a different way by now, but he was still a drifter who largely avoided politics and a steady job. His political views would develop later, but for now, he headed for Munich, Germany, with ideas about German superiority and hateful prejudices in his mind. ❧

4 GERMAN SOLDIER

❧❧❧

In Munich, Hitler rented a cheap room and began his usual routine of painting and selling pictures of the city's famous buildings. He liked to sit in cafés, reading newspapers and discussing current events with anyone who would listen. In February 1914, Austrian military authorities finally caught up with him and brought him back to Austria to serve in the Austro-Hungarian army. However, they found him too weak for military duty and did not make him serve.

Although he had not wanted to be part of the Austrian military, Hitler willingly volunteered for the German army when World War I suddenly started that summer. He finally had something he felt was worth fighting for—Germany.

The war started with the assassination of

The assassination of Archduke Franz Ferdinand and Archduchess Sophie of Austria thrust Europe into World War I in 1914.

Archduke Franz Ferdinand, the prince who was heir to the 84-year-old ruler of the Austro-Hungarian Empire. An extremist from Serbia shot Ferdinand and his wife Sophie while they were driving in their open car in Sarajevo, Bosnia, a territory that both Austria and Serbia claimed.

The archduke's assassination led Austria-Hungary to declare war on Serbia. Germany had vowed to stand by neighboring Austria-Hungary and now held true to its word. When Russia came to the aid of Serbia, Germany declared war on Russia. Then France decided to help Russia, and Germany declared war on France as well. Germany also turned against Belgium, which hadn't taken sides, but the route through that country was the quickest way to conquer the French capital of Paris. The United Kingdom honored its pledge to protect Belgium and thus declared war on Germany. Soon other countries joined the fight, and it became a worldwide war.

Since he was not a strong soldier, Hitler served as a messenger, carrying orders between commanding officers' underground bunkers and the troops in the trenches. He called his time as a soldier "the greatest and most unforgettable time of my earthly existence." Ten years later, he wrote about his war experience:

> *Even today I am not ashamed to say that, overpowered by stormy enthusiasm, I fell*

down on my knees and thanked heaven from an overflowing heart for granting me the good fortune of being permitted to live at this time. A fight for freedom had begun, mightier than the earth had ever seen.

Adolf Hitler in the crowd in Munich, Germany, during the mobilization of the German army for World War I

Hitler's war experience shaped the rest of his life. He recalled many years later that he had no worries during his six years in the army. He was well supplied with clothes, food, and a place to stay. But its importance went far beyond feeling well taken care of. Hitler would one day say:

It was with feelings of pure idealism that I set out for the front in 1914. Then we saw

> *thousands of wounded and dying. Thus*
> *I realized that life is a continuous cruel*
> *struggle, and has no other object but the*
> *preservation of the species. An individual*
> *can die, provided others live on.*

After just four days of fighting, Hitler wrote to friends in Munich that almost 3,000 of the 3,600 men in his regiment had been killed or wounded. In the face of such devastation, he started thinking about how important it was for Germans to survive. In a letter from the front, Hitler described how he disliked international peace and wanted only a pure Germany without any foreigners:

> *Those of us who are lucky enough to see*
> *our homeland again will find it purer*
> *and cleansed of affections for foreigners.*
> *... Our inner sympathies for international*
> *peace will also be broken. That will be*
> *worth more than any territorial gains.*

Although his fellow soldiers grew tired of the fighting and the stress of war, Hitler relished it. His military supervisor would sometimes need a message delivered in the middle of the night. He would call out "Messenger!" and Hitler would jump up. "You're always the one," said his supervisor. "Let the others sleep," Hitler replied. "I don't mind." Not all of Hitler's comrades appreciated his dedication, however. Many cursed him and found him unbearable.

Hitler's job was often dangerous. Later, he told how he narrowly escaped death several times. He described one instance when a bullet tore through the sleeve of his shirt but left him unharmed. In another instance, he told how he was eating in a trench with other soldiers when he was overcome with a feeling that he should move. Shortly after he found another place to eat, a shell burst over the trench where he had been sitting and killed everyone in the trench.

Adolf Hitler (right) with two other soldiers and Foxy, the military unit's pet dog, in April 1915

Adolf Hitler dressed in his World War I uniform, c. 1915

Hitler's close brushes with death proved to him that he was being saved for some bigger purpose in life.

Throughout much of World War I, Germany seemed on the verge of victory. It conquered Luxembourg, nearly all of Belgium, and the northern portion of France. To the east, Russia made a peace agreement with Germany in December 1917, giving Germany a vast amount of territory. However by 1918, the German army was exhausted, and supplies were difficult to find.

The United States had entered the fight in 1917. Unlike troops from other countries that had been fighting for three years, American soldiers were fresh and well supplied. By the summer of 1918, it was clear Germany could not win the war.

German citizens had grown tired of war. Revolts broke out across Germany. Sailors refused to take warships into battle. Workers in weapons factories went on strike, refusing to make more bombs and guns. Soldiers refused to listen to their officers, and the country's leader, Kaiser Wilhelm II, fled to the Netherlands. Anti-war leaders formed groups made up of workers and former soldiers and took over the government at the local level. However, they were unsuccessful on the national level.

Wilhelm II was the leader of Germany from 1888 to 1918, when he went into exile in the Netherlands.

On November 11, 1918, a delegate from Germany signed a truce, and fighting ceased. Soon after, the victorious powers—the Allies—met at Versailles, near Paris, France, to hammer out a peace treaty.

World War I had ravaged many parts of Europe. Millions had died. Cities, roads, bridges, factories, and farmlands had been destroyed. After suffering death and destruction of their own, the Allies had no intention of being charitable to the defeated Germans.

More than seven months later, on June 28, 1919, the Treaty of Versailles was finally signed. It had taken France, Britain, and the United States—called the Big Three—a long time to agree on what should be in the treaty.

Georges Clemenceau, prime minister of France,

wanted Germany punished so severely that it would never be able to start another war again. David Lloyd George, Great Britain's prime minister, also wanted Germany punished but was more worried about the spread of communism outside Russia. He feared that German citizens might prefer communism if the treaty was too harsh. However, George also realized his political career would quickly come to an end if he was too easy on Germany.

The last leader of the Big Three, U.S. President Woodrow Wilson, wanted to see Germany punished. But he also hoped the wounds of war could be healed. The treaty forced Germany to take sole responsibility for starting World War I. The Allies demanded that Germany pay about $33 billion in reparations, the cost of damages it had caused to other countries.

British Prime Minister David Lloyd George (left), Italian President Vittorio Orlando, French Prime Minister Georges Clemenceau, and U.S. President Woodrow Wilson stood outside the Hotel Crillon in Paris, France, before the Versailles Peace Conference in 1919.

Attempting to pay it would cripple Germany financially for many years.

The treaty also limited the German army to 100,000 men and forbade them from having an air force or owning tanks. Germany's navy could have just six battleships and no submarines. In addition, Germany was stripped of more than 13 percent of its territory—proportionally the same as taking away from the United States an area larger than California, Nevada, Oregon, and half of Washington. The land was given to France, Belgium, Denmark, Poland, and Czechoslovakia.

> *It would have taken many years for Germany to pay the huge reparation sum after World War I. Germany was given up to 60 years to pay it off, which meant it would pay until the 1980s. However, Germany stopped paying in 1931 during the Great Depression.*

Germans found the Treaty of Versailles harsh, unfair, and humiliating, but the Allies didn't care. Germany had no say in the proceedings. If the Germans failed to sign the treaty, the Allies would go back to waging war against them.

The Treaty of Versailles also established the League of Nations, an international organization founded to end any chance of another world war. However, the League didn't fulfill its lofty goal, and the treaty didn't secure peace in Europe. Instead, it set the stage for one angry German soldier—Adolf Hitler—to rise to power. 𝒮

5 GETTING INTO POLITICS

❧∽❧

When Germany surrendered on November 11, 1918, Hitler was in a hospital near Berlin recovering from temporary blindness caused by a mustard gas attack. News of Germany's defeat devastated him. He later wrote:

> Since the day when I had stood at the grave of my mother I had not wept until now. ... And so it had all been in vain. In vain all the sacrifices and privations; in vain the hunger and thirst of months which were often endless ...; and in vain the death of two millions who died. ... In these nights hatred grew in me, hatred towards all those responsible for this deed.

Hitler wanted to blame someone for the great

Adolf Hitler (back row, center) recovered with his fellow soldiers in a military hospital at the end of World War I.

suffering and death that led to Germany's downfall. At first, he didn't know whom to hate.

That month, he was released from the hospital. The war was over, and he was again without a goal in life. Still in the army, he traveled back to Munich, where he served as a guard for several months. After the kaiser had fled, Kurt Eisner, who was Jewish, became the leader of the German state of Bavaria's revolutionary communist-style government. Hitler hated the Socialists and Jews who were in charge, but he was so glad the kaiser was gone that he did nothing to oppose the new government. In fact, in February 1919, Hitler's regiment elected him to serve as a delegate to the Bavarian government.

Meanwhile, things in Germany were going downhill, and many of Hitler's army buddies began blaming this on Eisner and other Jews and Socialists in the government. Hitler blamed Jews, renewing his old prejudices against them from Vienna. He also blamed the Weimar Republic, Germany's first attempt at a democratic form of government. He claimed it was controlled by Jews, even though there were only a few Jews in the Cabinet and the *Reichstag*, Germany's lawmaking body.

At the end of April 1919, the Bavarian revolution was crushed. Hitler was assigned to question his fellow soldiers to find out who supported the new government. Then he took an educational course

Buildings were damaged in riots that broke out when the Communist Party of Germany tried to take control of Berlin, Germany, on January 31, 1919.

about the dangers of extreme socialism. The teacher noticed Hitler was a gifted speaker and asked him to teach soldiers why they shouldn't support socialism.

Soon the army assigned Hitler to talk with soldiers returning from the war who might sympathize with the communist cause. Hitler worked hard to create a hatred of communism among the soldiers. He also gave them someone else to blame for all their problems—Jews. As he talked to larger and larger groups, Hitler discovered he possessed a gift to persuade people through public speaking. His listeners agreed. One of them wrote:

> *Herr Hitler is … a born people's speaker,*
> *and by his fanaticism and his crowd appeal*
> *he clearly compels the attention of his lis-*
> *teners and makes them think his way.*

Hitler also served as a spy for the army. He began working to find groups that thought the army should be dissolved and that Germany should live in peace with other nations. One group he checked on was the tiny German Workers' Party (GWP). The organization was created by Anton Drexler, a German railroad employee who was trying to improve conditions for workers.

Anton Drexler, founder of the German Workers' Party, later called the National Socialist German Workers' Party—the Nazi Party

Hitler and 23 others attended a GWP meeting. Although Hitler didn't report that the group was a threat, his army superiors ordered him to attend a second meeting on September 12, 1919. About 40 people gathered to listen to a speaker whom Hitler found boring. However, Hitler was interested in the discussion that followed and even passionately responded to someone with whom he disagreed. This caught Drexler's attention. "This one has what it takes," Drexler said. "We could use him."

Drexler made sure Hitler received one of the group's pamphlets and asked him to come to another meeting. Hitler took the pamphlet back to his dirty room. That night, as was often the case, Hitler found it difficult to sleep. Waiting to drift off, he watched mice eating food he'd set out on the floor. "I had known so much poverty in my life that I was well able to imagine the hunger, and hence also the pleasure, of the little creatures," he said.

When the clock struck 5 A.M., Hitler was still awake. He reached for the pamphlet, titled "My Political Awakening." To his surprise, it interested him. It talked about a new political party that had been created for people who were upset with conditions in Germany. Even so, Hitler soon forgot about the pamphlet. But one day, he received a postcard that said he was accepted as a member of the GWP.

Although he had been toying with the idea of

starting his own political group, Hitler decided he wanted to attend another GWP meeting. It was illegal for members of the German army to join any political party, but Hitler's superiors felt his membership in the GWP could help him spy on the group. He was ordered to join.

Soon Hitler discovered that the organization gave him a place to tell other people about his own ideas. At his prodding, the GWP started holding meetings in bigger rooms so more people could attend. They sent out invitations and eventually scraped together enough money to advertise their meetings.

At the end of March 1920, Hitler left the army to concentrate more on his political ambitions. People were ready to hear his message, and he knew it. The German people had grown tired of the government's inability to improve their daily lives. Unemployment, poverty, and hunger were problems the government couldn't readily fix. Money was being sent to other countries to pay for war damages, but angry German citizens wanted this money to be used to help them out of their poverty and hunger. Their rage sparked riots.

Because of Hitler, the GWP became an important political force in Munich by 1921. Now it was called the National Socialist German Workers' Party— the Nazi Party, for short. The organization drew thousands to its rallies. People flocked to meetings especially to hear Hitler's passionate speeches.

Hitler knew he was important to the group and used his influence to gain more power. He threatened to resign from the Nazis unless he was named party chairman and allowed to make all the decisions. Knowing Hitler had caused the Nazi organization to grow, the group agreed. They also started calling him *Führer*, the German word for "leader."

Through speeches and newspaper articles, Hitler spread his message that openly criticized Germany's democratic government. He blamed the government, Jews, and communists for hardships the people of Germany were suffering. He also claimed that those groups were responsible for losing World War I. All Germans should join together to oppress Jews and communists and bring back national pride, he urged. Many Germans clung to Hitler's words. They wanted a strong leader to end the hard times and give them reasons to be proud of their country once again.

By 1922, other nations were beginning to worry about groups that were forming in Germany. In the fall, U.S. Army Captain Truman Smith was sent to Munich to find out more about Hitler and the Nazi Party. Smith talked with German government officials, generals, and Hitler's friends. After observing Hitler review his storm troopers at Nazi headquarters, Smith met with him. Hitler didn't hide his vision for Germany from his American visitor. "Only a dictatorship can bring Germany to its feet," he told Smith.

In his notebook, Smith described Hitler as a demagogue, a political leader who gains power by

Hitler spoke to a crowd that had gathered on February 28, 1923, in Munich, Germany.

appealing to people's emotions and agreeing with their prejudices. "I have rarely listened to such a logical and fanatical man. His power over the mob must be immense," Smith wrote.

In his long report about Hitler and the Nazi Party, Smith said Hitler could pose a threat to peace in the world. "I have the impression he's going to play a big part, and whether you like him or not he certainly knows what he wants," Smith concluded.

The report was filed away and forgotten by the U.S. State Department. Meanwhile, Hitler put his plan into action. He formed a private army called the *Sturm Abteilung* (Storm Section)—SA for short. On November 8, 1923, Hitler put his SA "brownshirts," as they were called, into action. They tried to take over the German government in what was later called the Beer Hall Putsch. Through the *putsch*, a German word meaning violent government takeover, Hitler planned first to control Bavaria, whose capital was Munich. Then with Bavarian soldiers under his control, he expected to take over the national capital—Berlin.

Hitler's army, the Sturm Abteilung (SA), was formed in 1921 to disrupt political meetings and to protect Hitler. The army wore grey jackets, brown shirts, ski caps, knee-length pants, thick woolen socks, combat boots, and a black armband. On the armband was a swastika, a Nazi symbol formed by a Greek cross with the four ends of the arms bent in a clockwise direction. They carried swastika flags and were accompanied by bands of musicians.

Rifles were distributed to Hitler's army outside Munich before the 1923 putsch.

At a Munich beer hall, about 3,000 people listened as Bavarian leaders spoke. Hitler quietly drank a beer in the back of the room. At 8:30 P.M., Hitler's SA arrived, and the putsch began. Nazis surrounded the building. Armed with guns, the brownshirts flooded the hall. Hitler and some of his associates made their way to the platform. At the podium, Hitler spoke:

> *I am going to fulfill the vow I made to myself five years ago when I was a blind cripple in the military hospital: to know neither rest nor peace until the November criminals have been overthrown, until on the ruins of the wretched Germany*

of today there should arise once more a Germany of power and greatness, of freedom and splendor.

When Hitler threatened to shoot everyone in the hall, the head of the Bavarian army, the chief of police, and the acting head of the government agreed to support Hitler and his armed followers. They were only pretending to cooperate, however.

While Hitler and his men held the Bavarians captive in the hall, other Nazis were assigned the task of taking over government buildings and arresting Bavarian officials. When a problem arose outside, Hitler left to resolve it. The general in charge at the hall was soon convinced that the captive Bavarian leaders were on Hitler's side, so he agreed to let them go. As soon as they were released, the men mobilized their forces to drive out the SA.

When he realized what had happened, Hitler flew into a rage. Troops loyal to the Bavarian government had now squared off against Hitler's troops. Hitler ordered thousands of his SA soldiers to march through downtown Munich. In a central square, a Nazi began firing at Bavarian police and touched off a gun battle. Several policemen and about 16 Nazis were killed. As bullets flew, Hitler's bodyguard threw himself on Hitler to protect him. The bodyguard was shot several times, probably saving Hitler's life. Hitler fled to a friend's home where he went into hiding.

Three days later, he was discovered and arrested.

After the failed putsch, Hitler was put on trial for treason. The trial attracted national attention and made Hitler famous throughout Germany. He was convicted but received a light sentence of five years at Landsberg Prison, about 30 miles (48 kilometers) west of Munich.

At first, Hitler was miserable. He felt betrayed by those he trusted and embarrassed by the way newspaper articles were poking fun at him and his failure. He was also in physical pain from dislocating his left shoulder during the putsch. Upset and depressed, Hitler refused to eat. By the time his old friend Anton Drexler visited him, Hitler hadn't eaten in almost two weeks. Drexler was surprised by Hitler's pale, thin appearance. "I found him sitting like a frozen thing at the barred window of his cell," he remembered.

The prison doctor told Drexler that Hitler would die if he didn't eat soon. For nearly two hours, Drexler tried to coax Hitler out of his depression. "I said he'd no right to give up all for lost, however bad things seemed," Drexler said. "The party would look to him to start it all up again someday ... at last I said how we'd all rather die than go on without him." Those words of loyalty broke the spell of Hitler's depression. Soon he was making plans for his future.

In 1924, while still in prison, he began writing his

*Hitler looking
out a barred
window in
Landsberg
Prison in 1924*

most famous work, *Mein Kampf*, which means my struggle. Along with giving information about himself, Hitler spewed out hatred against Jews in his book. He wrote that he believed Germans were superior to all others. He also shared his plan to destroy democratic countries and rid Europe of Jews. Officials in the United States and Great Britain were aware of *Mein Kampf*, but few really believed Hitler would or could put such plans into action. ❧

6 RISE TO POWER

☙❧

Because Hitler had won the sympathy of important government officials during his trial, his time in prison ended up more pleasant than it might have otherwise been. He received many requests from reporters and others who wanted to speak with him. His time in prison also made his hatred of Jews grow even deeper:

> *I have changed my opinion concerning the methods of fighting Jewry. I have come to the realization that I have been far too soft up to now! ... I have finally come to realize that the harshest methods of fighting must be employed in the future if we are to win. I am convinced that this is not only a matter of life and death for our people but for all peoples. The Jew is a world pest.*

Hitler left Landsberg Prison on December 20, 1924.

In 1924, Hitler got an early release from prison after serving just nine months of his five-year sentence. The Bavarian Supreme Court ordered his release. Hitler had won over everyone at Landsberg Prison. When he left, the warden and the prison staff were in tears. They didn't want him to go.

Faithful Nazi followers waited outside Hitler's Munich apartment to greet him when he arrived. Inside, Hitler found gifts of flowers and food. He immediately got back to work.

Early in 1925, Hitler met with Heinrich Held, the prime minister of Bavaria. He told Held that he wanted to help the government and vowed his undying loyalty. Held must have believed him, because five weeks later, Hitler and the Nazis were allowed to re-enter Bavarian politics.

On February 27, 1925, Hitler gave his first public speech since being released from prison. He spoke in the same beer hall where he had begun his rebellion. About 4,000 people crowded into the hall, and another 1,000 stood outside the overcrowded building. Hitler had become a hero to the Bavarian people.

Adolf Hitler believed he could gain more power through public speaking than by writing. In his case, it proved to be true. He recognized this early, writing about it in his 1924 book, Mein Kampf. He wrote, "I know that men are won over less by the written than by the spoken word, that every great movement on this earth owes its growth to great orators and not to great writers."

In his speech, Hitler called for a fight to the death against Jews and communists. He stirred up people's emotions and personal prejudices and gave them someone to blame for their suffering. Hitler's message was too strong for the Bavarian government, however, and he was banned from speaking in Bavaria for another two years. But he had planted the seeds for his future rise to power.

Hitler posed for a photo during the recording of one of his speeches after his release from Landsberg Prison.

Hitler now decided to change his strategy. Instead of a violent putsch against the heart of government, he would take control of Germany by creating a pyramid of local organizations all across the country. They would give the Nazi Party a broad power base. The party would work through these organizations until the Nazis were strong enough to take over complete power in Berlin. These local organizations were indeed established, but as long as life in Germany was going well, very few people paid much attention to them.

In the second half of the 1920s, Germany was again becoming a prosperous and respected country. In 1927, it became a full-fledged member of the League of Nations, which gave the country a say in international affairs. But Hitler's real chance at power came when the world's economy spiraled out of control after the great U.S. stock market crash of October 1929. Many Germans suffered financially when prices for stock shares on the New York Stock Exchange nose-dived. This reignited their anger about the money their country was paying in World War I damages.

At a time when banks were failing and unemployment was rising, a national election was held in Germany. If a chancellor didn't get a majority vote in the Reichstag, then national elections were held. These elections were becoming more frequent, and each time a national election was held, the Nazi Party did better. In 1924, the party had 3 percent support. But by 1930, its share of the votes jumped to 18 percent.

Hitler ran for president of Germany in 1932 and received an astonishing 30 percent of the votes. But it was not enough to win. Paul von Hindenburg was reelected. Hitler's strategy had taken him a long way, but he still did not have a majority of voters on his

Munich residents salute Adolf Hitler, leader of the National Socialist German Workers' (Nazi) Party, during his visit there in 1929.

Much of what we know about Hitler comes from his book, Mein Kampf. But his story is very much the way he wanted things to be and not necessarily the truth. As Hitler became famous, people wrote down their memories of him. Journalists and historians tried to find out all they could about him by looking at his school and army records, combing through newspapers, asking people for letters and drawings Hitler had sent them, and interviewing anyone Hitler had been in touch with. Hitler's sister Paula shared some information with the U.S. Army after her brother died. In order to write about Hitler's life, historians have to check all sources and decide which ones are true.

side. He would soon gain more supporters simply by his charm.

Many women were attracted to Hitler. Rich older women showed their appreciation of him by donating large sums of money to the Nazi Party. Younger women were also fascinated by this man who was quickly rising to power. Some were so taken by him that they became a danger to themselves.

Hitler's 20-year-old niece Geli was one of those women. Hitler's half-sister Angela started working as his housekeeper, and a few months later, her daughter Geli joined her. Soon Geli was accompanying the 39-year-old Hitler on trips and to official Nazi parties in Munich. Hitler's friends said that Geli was the only woman besides his mother that Hitler ever had deep feelings for.

But Hitler was a busy older man, and Geli was a much younger, lively girl. Hitler soon became very jealous and prohibited Geli from going out without chaperones. One day in 1931, while sad and depressed, she shot herself in the heart with Hitler's revolver and died.

Hitler was heartbroken. But a short time later, he became interested in another young woman, pretty 19-year-old Eva Braun, assistant to his personal photographer. Braun often complained bitterly that Hitler neglected her. In 1932, she also shot herself, but unlike Geli, she survived. Hitler paid a little more attention to her after that, but she attempted to take her own life again in 1935.

Eva Braun (1912-1945), was Adolf Hitler's mistress for many years. Hitler always carried this picture of her in his wallet.

Eva dreamed of marrying Hitler and starting a family, but Hitler considered himself married to Germany. He saw the German people as his children. They needed a father to lead them out of the desperate times they were suffering, he claimed. He believed he was that man. A wife and children would only get in the way of his plans for his beloved country.

Although Eva felt lonely and neglected, she never left him. Hitler felt some guilt about Eva's suicide attempts, but his devotion to Germany and his rise to power were more important to him. He was focused on becoming the country's leader.

In the summer of 1932, President Hindenburg flatly refused to choose Hitler as chancellor. Hitler said his party would have to have total control of the government, and Hindenburg wouldn't permit that. But conditions continued to get worse in Germany, and the other chancellors Hindenburg appointed failed to turn things around.

Although the aging Hindenburg

Germany's new government was called the Weimar Republic because the constitution was written in the city of Weimar. Delegates in the legislature, called the Reichstag, chose the chancellor, the head of the executive branch. The chancellor had to be confirmed by the Reich president, a largely ceremonial person like a king, but elected by popular vote. If the Reichstag deputies could not choose a chancellor, the president was empowered to appoint one. When the Reichstag was not able to choose its own candidate in January 1933, President Hindenburg appointed Hitler as chancellor.

didn't like Hitler, his advisers finally convinced him Hitler could do the job. On January 30, 1933, he named Hitler chancellor of Germany. It was a joyous day for many, although they didn't realize the horrors they would face because of this choice. Hans Frank, a Nazi Reichstag deputy, later recalled:

> *God knows our hearts were pure that day and if anyone had told us of the events to come, no one would have believed it, least of all I. It was a day of glory and happiness.* ☙

Paul von Hindenburg (1847–1934) was president of Germany from 1925 to 1934.

7 DICTATOR OF GERMANY

❦

After Adolf Hitler was named chancellor, he quickly made changes that would help him become the dictator of Germany. At first, he operated within German law. The constitution gave the president certain emergency powers. Hitler persuaded Hindenburg to use them to increase Hitler's control over the press and political meetings. Because Germany was no longer thriving under its present government, many leaders kept silent when Hitler started taking more control. They weren't sure at first how far Hitler would go, but they hoped he would use his power to help the people out of their misery.

In February 1933, an arsonist set fire to the Reichstag building. Hitler blamed the fire on the German Communist Party and had all of its deputies

On January 30, 1933, President Paul von Hindenburg handed over the rule of Germany to Nazi leader Adolf Hitler.

Members of the Nazi Party attended a rally at Nuremberg, Germany, in 1933, carrying standards bearing swastikas and the slogan Deutschland Erwache *(Germany Awake).*

arrested. He persuaded 85-year-old Hindenburg, who was often forgetful and confused, to take away many citizens' rights in order to prevent further uprisings. The German people no longer had freedom of speech or the right to assemble.

Under those conditions, the Nazi Party received 44 percent of the vote in a March 5, 1933, national election. Now Hitler worked to get absolute power for himself. He had the Reichstag vote on a law—the Enabling Act—that would essentially abolish the constitution. It would allow the executive as well as the legislative branch to make new laws. To persuade the Reichstag to approve the act, Nazi SA lined the walls of the building where parliament met to vote. The deputies of the Communist Party were in prison, so the only ones who dared to vote against the act were members of the old established Social Democratic Party. Their votes, however, were not enough to defeat the act. Now Hitler himself could decree laws.

The first law he passed eliminated the Communist and Social Democratic parties. Soon after, he banned all political parties except the Nazi Party. He also outlawed most non-Nazi organizations.

Hitler began to create a nation he could control completely. He abolished labor unions and shut down non-Nazi newspapers. German citizens could read only what Hitler and his new propaganda minister, Joseph Goebbels, wanted them to read. The Gestapo, Hitler's secret police, arrested anyone who protested against the government. Under Hitler's rule, mere suspicion was enough to imprison or shoot someone suspected of a crime. So many people were arrested that Germany's prisons

Joseph Goebbels (1847–1945), Germany's minister of enlightenment and propaganda, used the so-called big-lie technique of repeating a lie until it was taken to be the truth.

couldn't hold them. The Nazis created a network of huge prison camps, called concentration camps, to hold their opponents and presumed enemies.

While Hitler ruled with a heavy hand, he also worked hard to be admired by German citizens. He tried to improve their lives by creating new jobs. Although the German *autobahns*, a network of state-of-the-art highways crisscrossing the nation, had been planned and begun before Hitler came to power, Goebbels had the newspapers write that Hitler had designed them. The German people believed it.

Hitler used government money to sponsor Nazi organizations for veterans, teachers, and children. Among these groups was the Hitler Youth, which targeted children between the ages of 10 and 18. Boys and girls belonged to separate organizations, and trained for several hours after school. Boys trained for military service by practicing marching, grenade throwing, gas defense, pistol shooting, and other skills. Girls learned how to be good mothers but also had to be able to run fast, throw a ball, swim, complete a two-hour march, and make a bed.

Hitler believed that the future of Nazi Germany depended on its children. He considered the Hitler Youth program as important as school. Training children and strengthening their desire to fight should be developed in any possible way, he stated. When children joined the Hitler Youth, they were told that

A Hitler Youth
march in 1933

"from today onwards your life belongs to the Führer."
During the next three years, the Hitler Youth would
grow from 100,000 to 5 million members, which was
more than 60 percent of Germany's youth.

While Hitler worked to please the Aryan Germans,
he stepped up his persecution of Jewish Germans.

On April 1, 1933, the Nazi government called for a boycott of Jewish businesses across the country. It was followed days later by the first of about 400 laws that took away the rights of Jewish citizens.

Jews could no longer hold government jobs. Benefits to Jewish veterans of World War I were canceled. Jewish students were banned from attending public colleges and later all public schools. Jews could not own radios, and even their household pets were taken away. In the next five years, about 150,000 of Germany's 535,000 Jewish citizens would leave the country. Those who stayed would face even worse situations than the loss of civil rights.

While persecution of Jews increased, Hitler concentrated on building up Germany's military strength. This would take time, and he didn't want to move so quickly that other nations would be alarmed. At first Germany was still bound by the Treaty of Versailles, which limited the size of its army and navy. However, in October 1933, Hitler announced that Germany was pulling out of the League of Nations. This was his way of showing how much he hated the Treaty of Versailles and the way Germany had been treated because of it.

The German military was too weak to defend itself against stronger nations like France or Great Britain. Hitler decided to make a bold move anyway. Despite warnings from his generals, he called on

German troops to march into the Rhineland, the land along the Rhine River in western Germany. Under the Treaty of Versailles, Germany wasn't allowed to have troops in this strip of land along Germany's border with France and Belgium. But on March 9, 1936, about 25,000 German soldiers stood there, waiting to see what would happen. If the French attacked, Germany would reveal how weak it truly was. If that happened, Hitler knew he would have to "withdraw with our tails between our legs."

Hitler's bluff paid off. No troops attacked, and on March 12, Germany took control of the Rhineland without a shot being fired. The League of Nations merely condemned Germany for breaking the Treaty

In March 1936, German forces crossed the Rhine River to occupy the Rhineland.

of Versailles. The success of Hitler's plan led the German people to believe even more strongly that this man could lead their country back to greatness.

That summer, Germany hosted the Olympic Games in Berlin and concealed its growing anti-Semitism from the world. But after the Games, the situation for Jewish Germans became more dreadful. One Jewish teenager's attempt to fight back caused a terrible backlash. On November 7, 1938, Herschel Grynszpan, a 17-year-old Polish Jew who had grown up in Germany, shot a German official in Paris. Grynszpan was angry because the Germans had forced his family to leave their home and had put them on trains to Poland with 10,000 other Jews. At first, Polish officials allowed them into the country, but then they closed the border. Grynszpan's family

Seventeen-year-old Herschel Grynszpan was arrested in Paris where he shot German Ernst von Rath in 1938 at the German Embassy. He was released from a Paris prison two years later but seized again and taken to Germany. His fate remains unknown.

was forced to camp out at the border in tents in the cold November weather. Grynszpan told police:

> *Being a Jew is not a crime. I am not a dog. I have a right to live and the Jewish people have a right to exist on this earth. Wherever I have been I have been chased like an animal.*

Two days later, the German official died from the gunshot wound, and Hitler and his top aides gave the signal to attack Jewish citizens throughout Germany. Nazi SA men ransacked and burned hundreds of synagogues, the Jewish houses of worship. They plundered and destroyed more than 7,000 Jewish stores and many Jewish cemeteries.

The human toll was higher. In the first 48 hours alone, police reported that 36 Jewish Germans were killed and 36 more were in critical condition. Many more Jews committed suicide. About 30,000 were arrested and taken to concentration camps. Within a few weeks, more than 400 Jews had been murdered. Hundreds more died in the following months.

This night of fear and destruction came to be known as *Kristallnacht* (Crystal Night) named for the shimmering broken window glass that littered the downtown sidewalks. Many more Jewish people left Germany after that night of terror. Hitler acted as if he were angry about all the violence and destruction.

A worker
cleared broken
glass from a
Jewish shop in
Berlin following
the anti-Jewish
riots called
Kristallnacht.

But he knew about *Kristallnacht* before it happened; in fact, he had planned and encouraged it.

Meanwhile, Hitler continued to take control of bits and pieces of Europe, always promising the latest conquest would be his last. Many European leaders grew uncomfortable with the situation, but they tended to believe Hitler's empty promises. World War I was still fresh in their minds, and they didn't want to risk starting another major war.

While building Germany's military strength, Hitler made other countries fearful by pretending his army was larger than it really was. He gave foreign visitors tours of his airfields, which were filled with many bomber and fighter planes. In reality, he moved the same planes from airfield to airfield to make it seem as if he had more planes than he really did.

As he worked to fool other countries with his supposed military strength, Hitler set his sights on his next conquest—Poland. Great Britain and France had agreed to come to Poland's aid if Germany invaded, but Hitler doubted these countries would fulfill their promise.

In August 1939, the two most powerful dictators in the world—Hitler and the Soviet Union's Joseph Stalin—signed an alliance. Though Hitler hated the Soviet Union because it was a communist country, he knew he needed to form a temporary partnership with Stalin in order to take over Europe. Germany didn't want to face a serious fight against Russia to its east while fighting countries to the west.

Under a secret agreement, Stalin promised not to stand in the way of Hitler's plan to invade Poland. In return, Germany would leave half of Poland for the Soviets. With the alliance in place, Hitler prepared to overrun Poland. He'd soon see whether Great Britain and France would keep their promise and go to war to help his next target. ❧

8 AGAINST THE WORLD

❧

Until 1939, politicians around the world had convinced themselves that Hitler was mainly taking back territory that Germany had lost under the terms of the Versailles Treaty. However, when Germany invaded Poland on September 1, 1939, that illusion was shattered. Hitler was building a new empire, and Great Britain and France prepared to stop him.

World War II had begun.

Germany's mighty *blitzkrieg*, or "lightning war," made the invasion of Poland swift. With great speed and surprise, the German army took over Poland in less than a month. Hitler followed his victory in Poland by invading Norway, Denmark, Belgium, Luxembourg, and the Netherlands. By June 1940, France also fell into German hands.

Rubble and ruined buildings covered the streets after the German bombing of Warsaw, Poland, in September 1939.

While Germany tore through Europe, Hitler was at home, staying up late watching movies or talking with friends. Often he was up until about 3 A.M. and didn't rise until noon.

He stepped up his persecution of Jews in the countries he conquered. He required them to identify themselves by wearing a badge—a star of David with the word *Jude* (Jew) written inside. German soldiers and policemen forced Jews in Poland to leave their homes and possessions behind and move to walled areas called ghettos. Diseases soon spread in the tightly packed apartments of these overcrowded districts. Already weakened by hunger, thousands of Jews died.

Jewish citizens were required to wear the star of David to identify and distinguish them from the rest of society.

Life for Jewish citizens took an even more serious turn for the worse. Hitler began using his network of concentration camps to brutalize and murder people he thought were less valuable than Aryan Germans. First, he targeted Jewish Germans and the disabled, homeless, and unemployed. Then he included Jewish citizens in all of the countries allied with or conquered by Germany.

But soon, Hitler discovered that some countries weren't afraid to challenge him and the evil empire he had created. Hitler now faced trouble from the west. When France fell in 1940, Hitler expected Great Britain to make peace with Germany. But the British continued to fight, even though no other countries

On September 21, 1939, Nazi commanders in Poland were ordered to confine all Jews to areas called ghettos.

helped them.

Hitler made plans to invade Great Britain from the south. He realized that Britain's Royal Air Force (RAF) must be defeated before his troops could safely cross the English Channel. In July 1940, the Battle of Britain began. The German air force outnumbered the RAF, but Great Britain's air-defense system was strong. Radar stations warned the British of German air attacks, and the RAF was prepared for them. In May 1941, Hitler gave up his air attacks against Great Britain. He was never able to attack on land.

On June 22, 1941, Germany shocked Stalin and invaded the Soviet Union. Hitler had never planned to stay true to his agreement not to attack the massive country. Hitler wanted the land east of Germany so his country could expand, and he coveted Russia's wheat fields and oil supplies.

Hitler expected Russia to fall as quickly as other countries had, but he was in for a surprise. The country he had tricked into an alliance now began to stand up to the Nazi regime. Expecting the battle to be swift and finished before cold weather hit, the German army was unprepared for the icy Russian winter. Thousands of German soldiers died from the cold and lack of supplies.

Hitler blamed Italian dictator Benito Mussolini for Germany's problems in Russia. The attack on the Soviet Union was supposed to take place a month

earlier than it actually occurred, but it was delayed when Hitler needed to rescue Italy from its battle with Greece. That hadn't been part of Hitler's plan.

Hitler had underestimated the strength of the Soviet Union and England. Soon he would realize he had also misjudged the United States. Almost a year earlier, in the fall of 1940, Germany had signed the

Fighting in World War II took place throughout Europe, North Africa, and the Pacific. Axis powers led by Germany fought the Allies.

Tripartite Pact with Japan and Italy. In it, the three countries agreed to support each another against their enemies. When Japan bombed Pearl Harbor, Hawaii, on December 7, 1941, the United States automatically became an enemy of Germany. Four days later, on December 11, 1941, Germany declared war on the United States.

The declaration of war against the United States served another purpose besides honoring the pact with Japan. Hitler hoped Japan would keep the United States busy fighting while he continued to battle the Soviet Union. He didn't count on the United States focusing on defeating him.

In the spring and summer of 1942, the Germans again battled the Soviet Union. However, the Soviet army resisted heroically, and the central Asian winter again worked in the Soviets' favor. In November 1942, German troops found themselves trapped in the city of Stalingrad (present-day Volgograd). Despite his generals' pleas to surrender, Hitler angrily insisted that his army not give up. He believed his troops could take Stalingrad. He was mistaken. About 850,000 German soldiers were killed, and 91,000 were taken prisoner.

In 1943, the Soviet Union's Red Army was victorious time after time in its fight against the Germans. The Soviets successfully pushed the German army back 250 miles (400 km). Hitler had

A long line of German prisoners marched to prison camps in 1943, after Germany was defeated in Russia.

failed against Great Britain, and now he was defeated by the Soviet Union. But he still believed Germany would be victorious. He believed he would one day rule the world, including the United States. In 1943, he wrote in his personal notes:

> *The most important point of final victory will be the exclusion of the United States from world politics for all time and the destruction of their Jewish community.*

Completing the extermination of Jewish populations in Europe and the United States was as important to Hitler as beating the Soviets. However, some Jewish groups decided to fight back. ♦

9 IN SPITE OF DEFEAT

❧❧❧

In April 1943, Jews in Warsaw, the capital of Poland, rose up against the Nazis who were trying to round them up and send them to death camps. About 700 Jewish resisters used handmade and stolen weapons to fight against more than four times as many well-equipped German soldiers. They managed to kill several hundred and wound more than 1,000 Germans.

In 1944, instead of focusing all his efforts on military battles, Hitler increased his mass murder of Jews. From May to July, more than 500,000 Hungarian Jews were put on trains to the Auschwitz-Birkenau concentration camp, where they were killed with poison gas when they arrived.

Hitler and his top advisers were proud of

When Jewish citizens arrived by train at Auschwitz-Birkenau, many were sent directly to the gas chambers.

One Jewish business-man affected by the boycott of Jewish businesses in Germany was Otto Frank. In 1934, he moved his family to Amsterdam, the Netherlands, where he started a new job. In 1940, the Germans invaded the Netherlands. Two years later, the Franks went into hiding, where Otto's 13-year-old daughter, Anne Frank, began writing a diary of the events taking place around her. The Franks were captured in 1944 and sent to concentration camps, where Anne died in 1945. Her diary was published in 1947 and became one of the world's most widely read books. The first American edition, titled Anne Frank: The Diary of a Young Girl, was published in 1952.

murdering millions of Jewish families. Heinrich Himmler was commander of Hitler's elite troops, the SS. In an October 4, 1943, speech, Himmler had told the SS leaders that it was their duty to deal with the Jews because the general population couldn't stomach the job. He said to them:

> Most of you here know what it means when 100 corpses lie next to each other, when 500 lie there or when 1,000 are lined up. ... This is an honor roll in our history.

The Nazis believed mass murder was a glorious and decent thing to do.

Hitler always gave only verbal orders for genocide, the organized killing of a large number of people, and used euphemisms, or code phrases, such as "solving the Jewish question." Himmler, who was in charge of carrying out Hitler's orders, didn't hide the fact that Hitler was behind the plan. The extermination program was an open secret among government officials.

In January 1944, Himmler spoke to more than 250 high-ranking German officers in Poland. In his speech, he told them how Hitler had given him the task of killing Europe's Jews and that the "Jewish question" had now been solved. His audience responded with applause.

But not everyone in Hitler's inner circle agreed with him and his plans. Some were turning against him. Among those joining the resistance was Count Claus von Stauffenberg. At first, Stauffenberg supported Hitler and agreed with his takeovers of Austria and Czechoslovakia. He was even comfortable with Germany's conquest of France and the Netherlands. But he changed his mind about Hitler after the German army burned whole villages and killed civilians in its

The room where bodies were stored before being burned at Auschwitz-Birkenau concentration camp was converted into a gas chamber in 1941.

battles with the Soviet Union. Then Stauffenberg and some other officers decided the only way to stop Hitler was to kill him.

Shortly after turning against Hitler, Stauffenberg was badly injured when his car ran over a land mine. He lost an eye, his right hand, and two fingers on his left hand. But he survived. Once he recovered, he helped hatch a plot to kill the Führer.

On July 20, 1944, Stauffenberg attended a military briefing with Hitler and brought with him a bomb concealed in his briefcase. Making an excuse to leave the room, Stauffenberg left behind the briefcase that he had placed close to Hitler. While he was gone, the bomb went off, but Hitler escaped with relatively minor injuries. Someone had pushed the briefcase under the heavy conference table, and the table blocked the force of the blast.

As Hitler realized he could no longer trust his generals, he grew depressed. By the fall of 1944, the insomnia Hitler had suffered from for years grew worse. Stomach pains and headaches kept him from sleeping. With lack of sleep, his once sharp memory began to fail. Gone were the days when he could glance at a document and recall its details much later. Now he found it difficult to even remember names.

To ease his pain and sleeplessness, Hitler turned to his doctors, who prescribed medications, including cocaine. The pills he took for stomach pain contained

tiny amounts of strychnine and atropine, poisons that actually made his condition worse.

In early 1945, despite his failing health and certain military defeat, Hitler still remained hopeful that his situation would improve. "Our enemies are gathering all their forces for the final assault," Hitler said. "No game is lost until the final whistle."

Hitler vowed to fight to the very end. ⌘

Hitler was born in present-day Austria. He made his impact on the world from Nazi headquarters in Berlin, Germany, where he ordered the invasion of six neighboring countries.

Ein Volk, ein Reich, ein Führer!

10 DEATH OR CAPTURE

❦

Hitler kept waiting for a miracle. He expected his German scientists or inventors to create some new magnificent weapon that would swing the war in his country's favor. Or maybe Winston Churchill, the powerful prime minister of Great Britain, would die or lose favor with his people. If this leader of the Allies were stopped, perhaps Germany would win.

Hitler waited in his underground bunker in Berlin to hear the outcome of the war. He hoped for a miracle. In hiding, Hitler lost track of what was happening on the war front. Often confused, he sometimes gave orders to German troops that didn't even exist. Meanwhile, his enemies approached Berlin from the east and the west.

The western push had started the year before

with Operation Overlord, a massive invasion of France. On June 6, 1944—D-Day—more than 150,000 Allied troops landed on the beaches of Normandy and broke the Nazis' hold on western Europe. During the following months, Allied troops fought their way east through France and Belgium on their relentless march to Berlin.

Finally, it became clear to Hitler that Germany would lose. He criticized his leaders for failing him on the battlefield. When anyone talked of retreat, he became furious. He said, "The army has betrayed me, my generals are good for nothing."

On April 28, 1945, Hitler received news that Himmler was negotiating Germany's surrender to the Allies. He read the information without emotion and declared Himmler a traitor.

Hitler wondered how this war would end. He feared death less than what would happen if the Soviet army captured him. He decided he wouldn't be taken alive and made plans to kill himself, if necessary.

Heinrich Himmler (1900–1945) was head of the SS and one of the most powerful men in Nazi Germany. He was responsible for carrying out Hitler's order to exterminate all Jewish people.

Just before midnight, he gave Eva Braun her longtime wish and married her in his underground bunker. Hitler wore his military uniform, and Eva dressed in a long, black, silk gown. Their marriage, however, was short-lived.

Sometime after 3:30 P.M. on April 30, 1945, Hitler and Eva Braun went to their private suite in the underground bunker. There, Eva swallowed poison and died. Hitler bit down on a poison capsule and had himself shot at the same time.

A Russian soldier stands amid the rubble in Hitler's underground bunker, where Hitler and Eva Braun were said to have committed suicide.

Adolf Hitler was dead. Before he died, Hitler wrote his final will. He described in detail what should be done with his and Eva's bodies after their deaths. His instructions read:

> My wife and I choose to die in order to escape the shame of overthrow. ... It is our wish that our bodies be burned immediately.

His followers proceeded to obey his last wishes. They took Adolf and Eva's bodies out the emergency exit to Hitler's garden, poured gasoline on them, and set them on fire. When the fire died out, their remains were buried in a crater made by a bomb.

When Soviet troops reached Hitler's headquarters in May 1945, they discovered that Hitler had killed himself. "That snake Hitler is dead," Soviet Commander Georgy Zhukov said. "He shot himself, and they burned his corpse. We found his charred carcass."

The Hitlers weren't the only ones to commit suicide in the bunker. Earlier in April, Hitler had

---

Hitler wanted to kill every Jewish person in the world. He called his plan the "Final Solution of the Jewish question." Today it is called the Holocaust, which means "great destruction." Around 6 million Jewish men, women, and children were murdered under Hitler's program. In addition, Hitler had about 250,000 gypsies, 70,000 disabled, 9,000 homosexuals, and many political and religious leaders killed during the Nazi regime.

sent for his loyal press secretary, Joseph Goebbels, and his family. Goebbels' wife Magda knew they would never return to their home and instructed their nurse to pack for their bunker visit. Magda hid her thoughts from her six children.

Joseph Goebbels loved Hitler and didn't hesitate to follow him in death. In the bunker, Goebbels and Magda first poisoned their six children. The next day,

German Nazi propaganda minister, Paul Joseph Goebbels, with his wife and three of their six children

Goebbels ordered another Nazi to shoot him and his wife, which the man did.

> In the 1930s *Adolf Hitler* was one of the most famous men in the world. Time magazine named him *Man of the Year* in 1938. *Millions* of Germans adored him, and he had many admirers around the world. *By* the 1940s he was responsible for the murders of millions of people. *Many Germans* believed in him, but he would be internationally hated as the man who plunged the world into a horrifying global war. *He* was and is one of the best-known and most-studied people in all of history.

On May 8, 1945, Germany surrendered unconditionally, ending World War II in Europe. Allied troops liberated the survivors in Hitler's death camps, and the horrors committed by Hitler and the Nazis were exposed to the world.

In the Dachau concentration camp alone, about 32,000 starving prisoners were set free by Allied soldiers. Troops also found more than 3,000 dead bodies. About 4,000 prisoners were gravely ill—more than 2,000 of them died during the next few weeks. As additional information came out, the public learned of the horrific things that had been done to people who had been taken to the camps.

Hitler came frighteningly close to succeeding in his goal of killing all Jews in Europe. Nearly two out of three European Jews were killed during World War II.

The dictator of Nazi Germany was dead, but the memories of the darkness and devastation of his

regime live on. Many tried to heal the wounds Hitler caused. Others continue working to ensure that future generations learn of his unspeakable deeds and never allow them to happen again. ❧

Young survivors of the Dachau concentration camp cheered their American liberators at the end of World War II.

HITLER'S LIFE

1889

Born at
Braunau am Inn,
Austria-Hungary,
April 20

1903

His father Alois
dies in January

1905

Drops out
of school
at age 16

1900

1896

The Olympics Games
are held for the first
time in recent history
in Athens, Greece

1903

Brothers Orville and
Wilbur Wright successfully
fly a powered airplane

WORLD EVENTS

1907

Fails entrance exam at General School of Painting of the Vienna Academy of Fine Arts; his mother Klara dies in December

1908

Again fails entrance exam at art school

1910

Lives on the streets; moves into homeless shelter; paints postcards to sell

1910

1913

Henry Ford begins to use standard assembly lines to produce automobiles

1909

The National Association for the Advancement of Colored People (NAACP) is founded

HITLER'S LIFE

1914

Volunteers for
German army at
the outbreak of
World War I

1920

Leaves the
army in March;
helps form the
Nazi Party

1921

Demands to
be named Nazi
Party chairman
and is granted
unlimited power

1915

1916

German-born
physicist Albert
Einstein publishes
his general theory
of relativity

1920

American
women get the
right to vote

1922

The tomb of
Tutankhamen
is discovered
by British
archaeologist
Howard Carter

WORLD EVENTS

1923

Plan to take
over the German
government
fails; put on trial
and sentenced
to prison

1924

Begins writing
Mein Kampf;
released from
prison

1933

Named
chancellor
of Germany

1935

1923

Irish Civil
War ends

1926

Claude Monet
and Mary Cassat,
well-known
impressionist
painters, die

1929

The U.S.
stock exchange
collapses, and
severe worldwide
economic depres-
sion sets in

HITLER'S LIFE

1939

Orders German army to invade Poland; France and Great Britain declare war on Germany; World War II begins

1940

Orders occupation of Denmark, Holland, Belgium, Luxembourg, Norway, and France

1941

Begins killing non-Aryans; invades the Soviet Union; declares war on the United States

1940

1939

Dictator Francisco Franco conquers Madrid, ending the Spanish Civil War

1941

Japanese bombers attack Pearl Harbor, Hawaii, on December 7, and the United States enters World War II

WORLD EVENTS

1942

Uses concentration
camps to kill people
with poison gas

1944

Survives
assassination
attempt
in July

1945

Marries Eva
Braun; both
commit suicide
in underground
bunker in Berlin

1942

Japanese Americans are
placed in internment
camps because of fear
of disloyalty

1944

Operation Overlord,
code named D-Day,
begins with the
landing of 155,000
Allied troops on
the beaches of
Normandy, France

1945

The United
States drops
atomic bombs on
Hiroshima and
Nagasaki, Japan;
World War II ends

DATE OF BIRTH: April 20, 1889

BIRTHPLACE: Braunau am Inn, Austria-Hungary

FATHER: Alois Hitler (1837–1903)

MOTHER: Klara Hitler (1860–1907)

SIBLINGS: Edmund (1894–1900)
Paula (1896–1960)

EDUCATION: Dropped out of school at age 16

SPOUSE: Eva Braun (1912–1945)

DATE OF MARRIAGE: April 28, 1945

DATE OF DEATH: April 30, 1945

PLACE OF BURIAL: Partially cremated in Berlin; remains placed in hole made by a bomb; later exhumed, recremated, and scattered

FURTHER READING

Ambrose, Stephen E. *The Good Fight: How World War II Was Won.* New York: Atheneum, 2001.

Dufner, Annette. *The Rise of Adolf Hitler.* San Diego: Greenhaven Press, 2003.

Giblin, James Cross. *The Life and Death of Adolf Hitler.* New York: Clarion Books, 2002.

Heyes, Eileen. *Adolf Hitler.* Brookfield, Conn.: Millbrook Press, 1994.

Nardo, Don. *Adolf Hitler.* San Diego: Lucent Books, 2003.

Warren, Andrea. *Surviving Hitler: A Boy in the Nazi Death Camps.* New York: HarperCollins Publishers, 2001.

LOOK FOR MORE SIGNATURE LIVES BOOKS ABOUT THIS ERA:

Benazir Bhutto: *Pakistani Prime Minister and Activist*
ISBN 0-7565-1578-5

Fidel Castro: *Leader of Communist Cuba*
ISBN 0-7565-1580-7

Winston Churchill: *British Soldier, Writer, Statesman*
ISBN 0-7565-1582-3

Jane Goodall: *Legendary Primatologist*
ISBN 0-7565-1590-4

Queen Noor: *American-born Queen of Jordan*
ISBN 0-7565-1595-5

Eva Perón: *First Lady of Argentina*
ISBN 0-7565-1585-8

Joseph Stalin: *Dictator of the Soviet Union*
ISBN 0-7565-1597-1

ON THE WEB

For more information on *Adolf Hitler*, use FactHound.

1. Go to *www.facthound.com*
2. Type in a search word related to this book or this book ID: 0756515890
3. Click on the *Fetch It* button.

FactHound will fetch the best Web sites for you.

HISTORIC SITES

United States Holocaust
Memorial Museum
100 Raoul Wallenberg Place S.W.
Washington, DC 20024-2126
202/488-0400
Displays of the Holocaust through exhibits and films

National World War II Memorial
National Mall
Washington, D.C.
800/639-4992
Honors the 16 million who served in the U.S. armed forces and the more than 400,000 who died in World War II

anti-Semitism
discrimination against Jews, because of their cultural background, religion, or race

Aryan
a term used by Nazis to describe a supposed master race of non-Jewish, pure-blooded Germans with blond hair and blue eyes

boycotts
refusals to do business with someone as a form of protest

dictator
a ruler who takes complete control of a country, often unjustly

euphemisms
the substitution of an offensive term with one that is not offensive

genocide
the organized killing of a large number of people

Holocaust
during World War II, the mass murder of millions of Jews, as well as gypsies, the disabled, homosexuals, and political and religious leaders

propaganda
information or ideas, some true and some untrue, which are deliberately spread among the public to try to influence their thinking

Reich
an empire or combination of several kingdoms

reparations
the payments of damages caused to another person's property

Source Notes

Chapter 1

Page 10, line 6: Duff Hart-Davis. *Hitler's Games: The 1936 Olympics*. New York: Harper & Row, 1986, p. 47.

Page 13, line 24: Ibid., p. 177.

Page 14, line 4: Ibid.

Page 14, line 11: William L. Shirer. *Berlin Diary: The Journal of a Foreign Correspondent, 1934–1941*. New York: A.A. Knopf, 1941, p. 65.

Chapter 2

Page 19, line 1: Ian Kershaw. *Hitler, 1889–1936: Hubris*. New York: W.W. Norton, 1998, p. 13.

Page 20, line 2: Adolf Hitler. *Mein Kampf*. Boston: Houghton Mifflin Company, 1971, p. 8.

Page 20, line 10: Ibid., p. 10.

Page 20, line 18: Ibid.

Chapter 3

Page 25, line 1: Ibid., p. 18.

Page 25, line 18: Ibid., p. 28.

Page 27, line 14: Ibid., p. 125.

Chapter 4

Page 30, line 23: Ibid., p. 163.

Page 30, line 26: Ibid., p. 161.

Page 31, line 12: Werner Jochmann (ed.). *Monologe im Führer-Hauptquartier 1941–1944* (trans. Harold Marcuse). Hamburg: A. Knaus, 1980, p. 71.

Page 32, line 14: Eberhard Jäckel, and Axel Kuhn. *Hitler: Sämtliche Aufzeichnungen 1905–1924* (trans. Harold Marcuse). Stuttgart: DVA, 1980, p. 69.

Page 32, line 24: Anton Joachimsthaler. *Adolf Hitler, 1880–1920: Korrektur einer Biographie* (trans. Harold Marcuse). Munich: Herbig, 1989, p. 127.

Chapter 5

Page 39, line 6: *Mein Kampf*, p. 206.

Page 42, line 2: *Hitler, 1889–1936: Hubris*, p. 124.

Page 43, line 9: John Toland. *Adolf Hitler*. Volume I. Garden City, N.Y.: Doubleday, 1976, p. 92.

Page 43, line 16: *Mein Kampf*, p. 220.

Page 46, line 11: *Adolf Hitler* (Toland). Volume I, p. 134.

Page 47, line 2: Ibid.

Page 47, line 7: Ibid., pp. 134–135.

Page 48, line 8: Ibid., p. 166.

Page 50, line 16: Ibid., p. 190.

Page 50, line 21: Ibid., p. 191.

Chapter 6

Page 53, line 8: Ibid., p. 210.

Page 61, line 16: Joshua Rubenstein. *Adolf Hitler*. New York: Franklin Watts, 1982, p. 51.

Chapter 7

Page 67, line 1: Ian Kershaw. *The "Hitler Myth": Image and Reality in the Third Reich*. Oxford: Oxford University Press, 1987, p. 208.

Page 69, line 9: *Adolf Hitler* (Toland). Volume I, p. 408.

Page 71, line 3: John Toland. *Adolf Hitler*. Volume II. Garden City, N.Y.: Doubleday, 1976, pp. 588–589.

Chapter 8

Page 81, line 6: Ibid., p. 876.

Chapter 9

Page 84, line 10: "Himmler's October 4, 1943, Posen Speech 'Extermination.'" *The Nizkor Project*. 29 Nov. 2005. www.nizkor.org/hweb/people/h/himmler-heinrich/posen/oct-04-43/ausrottung-transl-imt.html.

Page 87, line 5: *Adolf Hitler* (Toland). Volume II, p. 958.

Chapter 10

Page 90, line 11: Ibid., p. 983.

Page 92, line 5: Ibid., p. 997.

Page 92, line 20: Nikita Khrushchev. *Khrushchev Remembers*. Boston: Little, Brown, 1970, p. 219.

Fest, Joachim C. *Hitler*. New York: Vintage Books, 1974.

Fuchs, Thomas. *A Concise Biography of Adolf Hitler*. New York: Berkley Books, 2000.

Hitler, Adolph. *Mein Kampf*. Boston: Houghton Mifflin Company, 1971.

Jochmann, Werner (ed.). *Monologe im Führer-Hauptquartier 1941–1944*. Trans. Harold Marcuse. Hamburg: A. Knaus, 1980.

Kershaw, Ian. *Hitler: 1889–1936 Hubris*. New York: W.W. Norton & Company, 1998.

Kershaw, Ian. *Hitler: 1936–1945 Nemesis*. New York: W.W. Norton & Company, 2000.

Kershaw, Ian. *The "Hitler Myth": Image and Reality in the Third Reich*. Oxford: Oxford University Press, 1987.

Khrushchev, Nikita. *Khrushchev Remembers*. Boston: Little, Brown, 1970.

Shirer, William L. *Berlin Diary: The Journal of a Foreign Correspondent, 1934–1941*. New York: A.A. Knopf, 1941.

Shirer, William L. *The Rise and Fall of the Third Reich: A History of Nazi Germany*. New York: Simon & Schuster, 1988.

Toland, John. *Adolf Hitler*. 2 Volumes. Garden City, N.Y.: Doubleday, 1976.

Wiesel, Elie. "Adolf Hitler." *Time*, April 13, 1998. 22 Nov. 2005. www.time.com/time/time100/leaders/profile/hitler.html.

Brenda Haugen started in the newspaper business and had a career as an award-winning journalist before finding her niche as an author. Since then, she has written and edited many books, most of them for children. A graduate of the University of North Dakota in Grand Forks, Brenda lives in North Dakota with her family.

Image Credits

Hulton Archive/Getty Images, cover (top), 4–5, 16, 33, 34, 38, 41, 51, 52, 57, 64, 65, 67, 72, 74, 90, 96 (top left), 98 (top), 99 (top left), 100 (top); Hulton-Deutsch Collection/Corbis, cover (bottom), 2, 11, 12, 101 (top right); Fox Photos/Getty Images, 8, 69, 93; Bettmann/Corbis, 15, 76; Three Lions/Getty Images, 18, 21, 97 (top left); Hugo Jaeger/Timepix/Time Life Pictures/Getty Images, 19, 45, 96 (top middle); Courtesy of Snyder's Treasures, 22, 97 (top middle); Time Life Pictures/Pix Inc./Getty Images, 24; Behrouz Mehri/AFP/Getty Images, 26; The Granger Collection, New York, 28; Time Life Pictures/Mansell/Getty Images, 31; Keystone/Getty Images, 35, 42, 46, 48, 59, 62, 77, 81, 99 (top right); Lee Jackson/Topical Press Agency/Getty Images, 36; Heinrich Hoffmann/Getty Images, 55; General Photographic Agency/Getty Images, 61; Central Press/Getty Images, 70; The Holocaust Martyrs' and Heroes' Remembrance Authority/ Yad Vashem/FA-268/35, 82, 101 (top left); Michael St. Maur Sheil/Corbis, 85; Mary Evans Picture Library, 88; William Vandivert/Time Life Pictures/ Getty Images, 91; Horace Abrahams/Keystone/Getty Images, 95; Compass Point Books, 96 (bottom left); NASA, 96 (bottom right); Library of Congress, 97 (bottom), 98 (bottom both); Corel, 99 (bottom left); DVIC/ NARA, 100 (bottom), 101 (bottom right); Clem Alberts/DVIC, 101 (bottom left).